SWEET RIDES

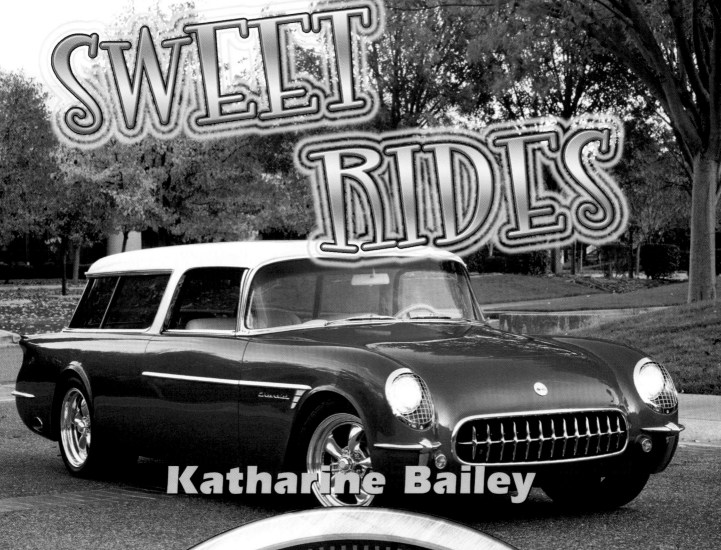

Katharine Bailey

x1000r/min

CRABTREE PUBLISHING COMPANY
www.crabtreebooks.com

Crabtree Publishing Company
www.crabtreebooks.com

To Matt Houghton, for his patience and guidance in all of my writing endeavours.

Coordinating editor: Ellen Rodger
Series and project editor: Rachel Eagen
Editors: Carrie Gleason, Adrianna Morganelli, L. Michelle Nielsen
Design and production coordinator: Rosie Gowsell
Cover design and production assistance: Samara Parent
Art direction: Rob MacGregor
Scanning technician: Arlene Arch-Wilson
Photo research: Allison Napier

Consultant: Norm Mort, automotive historian and journalist

Photo Credits: AP /Wide World Photo: p. 25 (top); Blackhawk Auto Museum, Danville, CA, USA, Wolfgang Neeb/The Bridgeman Art Library International: p. 27 (bottom); Private Collection, Archives Charmet/The Bridgeman Art Library International: p. 7 (top); Private Collection/The Bridgeman Art Library International: p. 9 (top); Henny Ray Abrams/Reuters/Corbis: p. 11 (bottom); Bettmann/Corbis: p. 8, p. 24 (bottom), p. 31 (top); Corbis: p. 6 (top), p. 7 (bottom), p. 9 (bottom), p. 30, p. 31 (bottom); Daimler Chrysler/Reuters/Corbis: p. 13 (top); Andrew Fox/Corbis/Corbis: p. 12 (middle); Catherine Karnow/Corbis: p. 10; Kridler Charles/Cornis Sygma: p. 26 (bottom); Owaki - Kulla/Corbis: p. 11 (top); Carl & Ann Purcell/Corbis: p. 29 (top); Reuters/Corbis: p. 26 (top), p. 27 (top); Leonard de Selva/Corbis: p. 24 (top); Ted Soqui/Corbis: p. 25 (bottom); Yassukovich/Corbis/Sygma: p. 28 (bottom); Peter Yates/Corbis: p. 12 (bottom); Ron Kimball/Ron Kimball Stock: cover, p. 1, p. 4 (bottom), p. 5, p. 6 (bottom), p. 12 (top), p. 13 (bottom), p. 14, p. 15 (both), p. 16 (top), p. 18 (both), p. 19 (all), p. 21 (both), p.22 (both), p. 23 (both), p. 25 (middle), p. 28 (top), p. 29 (both); Sara Sherman/istock International: p. 2; Nick Morganelli: icon on all pages, p. 4 (top), p. 13 (middle). Other images from stock CD.

Cover: Ferrari continues to produce some of the sweetest sports cars, including this 2003 model.

Title page: Restored classics grab attention with flashy rims and stunning paint jobs, as seen on this 1954 Corvette Nomad wagon.

Library and Archives Canada Cataloguing in Publication

Bailey, Katharine, 1980-
    Sweet rides / Katharine Bailey.
(Automania!)
Includes index.
ISBN-13: 978-0-7787-3008-8 (bound)
ISBN-10: 0-7787-3008-5 (bound)
ISBN-13: 978-0-7787-3030-9 (pbk)
ISBN-10: 0-7787-3030-1 (pbk)

    1. Sports cars--Juvenile literature. 2. Sport utility vehicles--Juvenile literature. 3. Limousines--Juvenile literature. 4. Automobiles--Juvenile literature. I. Title. II. Series.
TL236.B33 2006   j629.222   C2006-902458-8

Library of Congress Cataloging-in-Publication Data

Bailey, Katharine, 1980-
    Sweet rides / written by Katharine Bailey.
        p. cm. -- (Automania!)
    Includes index.
    ISBN-13: 978-0-7787-3008-8 (rlb)
    ISBN-10: 0-7787-3008-5 (rlb)
    ISBN-13: 978-0-7787-3030-9 (pbk)
    ISBN-10: 0-7787-3030-1 (pbk)
    1. Sports cars--Juvenile literature. 2. Limousines--Juvenile literature. 3. Automobiles--Juvenile literature. I. Title. II. Series.
    TL236.B33 2006
    629.222--dc22
                                                        2006014366

Crabtree Publishing Company

www.crabtreebooks.com   1-800-387-7650

Published in Canada
Crabtree Publishing
616 Welland Ave.
St. Catharines, ON
L2M 5V6

Published in the United States
Crabtree Publishing
PMB16A
350 Fifth Ave., Suite 3308
New York, NY 10118

Published in the United Kingdom
Crabtree Publishing
White Cross Mills
High Town, Lancaster
LA1 4XS

Published in Australia
Crabtree Publishing
386 Mt. Alexander Rd.
Ascot Vale (Melbourne)
VIC 3032

Contents

Sweet on the Street

Sweet rides are valuable, attractive vehicles. They have distinctive styling, cool accessories, and high performance. Sweet rides are more than just vehicles for getting from place to place. They are expensive machines that turn heads and stand out in a crowd.

Nice Ride!

Sweet rides get noticed because they are less common than other cars. They are often made and sold in limited numbers, which makes them exclusive, or rare, and valuable. People buy sweet rides to show off their status, or importance in a community, and wealth. Sweet rides may be **customized** to express personal taste and style. They are designed to be eye-catching, and often have exceptional performance.

Sporty rides, such as a vintage Aston Martin (below), or a Ferrari (above), attract attention and offer excitement to drivers and passengers.

Rides of All Kinds

There are many types of sweet rides. A luxury car is an expensive vehicle that includes cool accessories and features a smooth, powerful ride. A sports car has a lightweight body and powerful engine, which helps the car go fast. Sport-utility vehicles, or SUVs, are larger than average cars. Many SUVs have similar features as, and performance like luxury cars, but they have more interior space for passengers or cargo. A retro ride is a new model of an older vehicle that was once very popular. Retro rides are modernized with new, trendy designs and include updated technology, such as modern braking and handling systems, and **satellite radio** or **global positioning systems (GPS)**.

This Rolls-Royce Silver Ghost Boattail Speedster was made in 1924. Rolls-Royce cars have been considered status symbols for nearly a century. They are rare, expensive, and are sure to turn heads on the street.

5

The War Years

The first sweet rides were the luxury cars of the early 1900s. The 1920s and 1930s are often said to be the most glamorous years in automotive history. This era ended abruptly when World War II broke out in Europe in 1939.

The Great Depression

The automotive industry in the United States and Europe was very successful in the 1920s. The invention of the **assembly line** meant that many cars could be made in a factory quickly. This made cars less expensive to make, which lowered prices, and led to more people being able to afford them. When the **Great Depression** struck in 1929, many people in Europe and the United States lost their jobs. People could barely afford food to feed their families, and did not have money for larger expenses such as cars. Despite the drop in sales during the 1930s, luxury cars were still made. Classic luxury cars from the 1930s include the Rolls-Royce Phantom II, Duesenberg SJ, and V12 Hispano-Suiza. These cars were very expensive, and were purchased by royalty, politicians, and celebrities.

(above) B-24 bombers were built at the Willow Run Plant in Michigan during World War II. The plant was built by Ford Motor Company.

(below) In the 1930s, people could customize their cars by asking for specific features and body designs. This particular Duesenberg from 1934 had long, sweeping fenders that stretched from the front of the car to the back.

The Bigger The Better

Luxury cars of the 1920s and 1930s were often very large. Their engines were big and powerful and took up a lot of room, which meant the hood, or the cover over the engine compartment, had to be long. These cars usually had large **chrome grilles** on the front, which protected the radiator. The radiator is a device that cools the engine.

Car Production Halts

World War II caused car production to stop in many European factories, and eventually in North American factories, too. World War II was a massive war, fought mostly in Europe and Asia from 1939 to 1945. The United States and Canada participated by sending their armies to fight overseas. Some American and European car companies began making war equipment, such as airplane engines, Jeeps, and tanks, rather than cars. This was because fighter planes and tanks were in much higher demand than cars.

(above) French car manufacturer Bugatti Motor Cars made some of the best sports cars of the era. This advertisement from 1929 is aimed at the wealthy who could afford to buy these expensive cars.

Women Go to Work

World War II caused many changes in North America, even though the fighting took place overseas. People were forced to **ration** goods, including food and gasoline. Many women went to work, replacing the male work force in automotive factories. This photo shows a woman working at a car wheel manufacturer in New York.

The Golden Age

The end of the war in 1945 brought more changes to North America and Europe. Factories began producing cars again, and by the early 1950s, people had more money to spend on luxury items, including cars.

American Recovery

Soldiers returned from the war overseas and began working at new jobs. The car companies who had built military equipment during the war returned to making vehicles once the war was over. New production methods and materials invented during the war made car manufacturing faster and more efficient. Families had more money and many people started buying houses as well as other expensive items. Car sales in North America increased significantly in the 1950s.

Europe Rebuilds

It took longer for the automotive industry to recover in Europe. Many companies had to rebuild factories that had been bombed and destroyed in the war, as well as repair damaged roads. Europe began **exporting** cars to North America to meet the demand there.

Workers examine newly assembled Buick cars as they roll off of the assembly line at a factory in Flint, Michigan.

Advertising

The amount of car advertising increased after the war. Advertisements in magazines, as well as billboards, and radio and television commercials showcased new cars. Advertisements and commercials urged people to buy a new car every year. Cars were thought to indicate a person's importance in society. A car became a status symbol and showed off a person's wealth. People desiring the latest trends in performance and style replaced their older vehicles with new ones.

New Look! New Life (V8 OR 6)! New Everything!

1955 CHEVROLET

(above) When World War II ended, advertisements portrayed cars as the key to happiness and success. People had money and needed new cars.

A man stands next to an old tire-making machine from the early 1900s. The first inflatable tires had a canvas inner tube that was surrounded by an outer leather layer.

Luxury Rides

A luxury car is the ultimate sweet ride. Luxury cars are stylish, comfortable, powerful, and expensive. They are often produced in limited numbers, making them exclusive and desirable.

The Price of Luxury

Luxury cars cost much more than regular cars. Some companies, such as BMW, make a range of cars that come with different price tags. Others, such as Rolls-Royce, specialize in a couple of models that are very expensive. Today's luxury cars come in many different sizes. They do not always have large hoods like the original luxury cars because the modern **V8** engine can produce more power in a compact shape. **Suspensions** on luxury cars are designed for a smooth ride.

Rides Like a Dream

Modern luxury cars are equipped with many accessories. They may include self-closing doors, keyless ignition, and different temperature zones for each passenger in the car. Some luxury cars even have refrigerators, flat-screen televisions, and expensive sound systems.

A wealthy man displays his collection of luxury cars.

Classy Cadillac

Cadillac is one of America's top luxury car brands. The company was founded in 1902 in Detroit, Michigan. Cadillacs of the 1950s reflected the excitement over cars in postwar America. They looked flashy and futuristic, featuring shiny chrome front grilles and tail fins with chrome-accented rear lights that were shaped like bullets. This futuristic design was popular for a short time and disappeared in the early 1960s.

Luxurious Lincoln

Lincoln is an American luxury car brand made by the Ford Motor Company. Lincolns are large, expensive cars that were originally designed for the wealthy, politicians, and celebrities of the glamorous 1920s and 1930s. Lincoln models such as the Town Car, the Continental, and the Mark VIII are known for their smooth handling and quiet ride. The 2006 Zephyr features a suspension that is tuned to handle like a sports car but gives the smooth ride of a luxury car.

(below) The Lincoln Zephyr was discontinued in 1942, but was reintroduced in 2006. The 2007 model, called the MKZ, looks different and features a larger engine than the Zephyr.

Tail Fins

Tail fins were a styling craze of the 1950s. Tail fins were located on the rear panels of a car. They stick out further than the trunk of the car in a triangular shape, like the fins of a fish or a jet. Tail fins were inspired by the look of jet airplanes. Cadillacs were the first cars to have tail fins. They were also known for having chrome accents and "wraparound" windshields that curved around the sides of the cars.

Rolls-Royce

English car manufacturer Rolls-Royce has created some of the most luxurious cars in the world. Rolls-Royce cars are very distinctive, featuring long hoods and large, square front grilles. The Silver Ghost was made from 1907 to 1925. Its smooth, quiet ride was advanced for the time. The 2006 Rolls-Royce Phantom has several luxury options that buyers can add at extra cost. These options include customized leather interiors, mini refrigerators, fold-down tables, and individual television screens for passengers.

Jumpin' Jaguars!

Jaguar cars are sleek and powerful like the wild cat they are named after. Jaguar was founded in 1922 in Blackpool, England, and was originally called the Swallow Sidecar Company. The company made sidecars, which are one-wheeled devices that hitch to the side of motorcycles to seat an extra passenger. The company debuted a luxury model called the SS Jaguar in 1936, and became Jaguar Cars Limited in 1945. Jaguars are elegantly designed with distinctive front ends. Many models feature long, smooth hoods that sweep down into small, round dual headlights.

(below) The Jaguar S-Type is a popular model.

(upper left) The Rolls-Royce hood ornament, the "Spirit of Ecstasy," was first used in 1911.

(above) Some luxury rides feature GPS, which provide drivers with maps to help get them from place to place.

The Lady Mercedes

Mercedes-Benz is a German brand of luxury car. It was originally two separate companies, one owned by a carmaker named Gottleib Daimler, and the other owned by an engineer named Karl Benz. The two companies joined and became Mercedes-Benz in 1926. The S-Class line includes some of the most popular Mercedes-Benz models. The line features the S600, a powerful vehicle with leather interior, deluxe sound system, and the latest technology.

Beautiful BMW

The letters BMW stand for Bavarian Motor Works, a German car manufacturer known for a wide range of high quality vehicles. The 7-Series is BMW's top line of modern luxury **sedans**. The 760Li is the most luxurious and powerful model in the 7-Series line. It includes a high **horsepower** engine and fancy interior options, such as a mini refrigerator and massaging seats. The BMW Z3 roadster gained fame as James Bond's car in the 1995 movie *GoldenEye*.

(below) BMW did not start making vehicles until 1928. BMW cars offer a smooth, stylish ride.

(bottom) Mercedes-Benz cars reach fast speeds with their high horsepower engines.

(above) The plush interior of a Mercedes-Benz S-Class car.

Sporty Rides

Sports cars are fast, expensive vehicles with powerful engines and eye-catching, aerodynamic **designs. They give people the feeling of driving a race car.**

Lightning Quick

Most sports cars have two doors and only two seats. They are smaller than average cars and are made with lightweight materials that reduce the cars' weight to help them go faster. A sports car often has a stiffer suspension to improve the handling of the car. A stiffer suspension makes the ride feel bumpier, but it helps the car stay on the road when taking corners at high speeds. Many sports cars are made in limited numbers, which makes them more valuable.

Check Out the Corvette!

Original design and a powerful engine define the Chevrolet Corvette. The first " 'Vette" was built in 1953. It was one of the first cars to have a **fiberglass** body, which made it both lightweight and strong. European sports cars dominated racing in the 1950s. Chevrolet's Corvette was built to rival European models and offer people a stylish car made in the United States. The Corvette became successful on the racetrack and was instantly popular in **dealerships**.

Sports cars, like this 1976 Corvette Stingray, are more expensive than regular cars because they are built in smaller numbers, and usually with more advanced technology. They feature powerful engines, wider tires, and bucket seats.

Wild Horses: The Mustang

The Ford Mustang was immediately popular when it debuted in 1964. The car was first available as a **convertible** with a **hardtop**. A fastback model became available later. The fastback had a roof that sloped down almost to the tip of the trunk, inspired by the aerodynamic race car designs of the day. The Mustang came with the GT option package, which is a set of features that can be added to a base model, or regular version of a car. The GT option included a more powerful V8 engine and dual exhaust pipes.

(above) The Ford Mustang created a new class of car called the pony car. It had a powerful engine packed into a smaller, sporty body.

American Muscle: The Camaro

(above) The IROC-Z Camaro included a heavy-duty suspension for high-speed handling, special decals, and a high-performance engine.

The Chevrolet Camaro was one of America's most recognizable sports cars. It debuted in 1967. Later Camaros featured the T-Top, which had a bar shaped like a "T" that divided the roof in left and right halves. This styling feature was also seen on Corvettes. The Camaro also had hood scoops, or raised vents, to allow cooling air to flow into the engine, and big, bold racing stripes on the hood. Early Camaros had a bulky body shape with a long hood, short passenger compartments, and a short trunk. They also featured large, rectangular grilles that ran the width of the car's front. Camaros have long bodies and ride lower to the ground than most cars.

A Wee Thing: The MG

The initials MG stand for Morris Garages, a dealership that sold the Morris brand of cars in England. Cecil Kimber, a Morris Garages employee, customized some of the Morris cars they sold and turned them into sporty MGs. Traditional MGs are compact, two-seat convertibles. They are known for being small, lightweight, and fast. Two of the most popular models are the MGA and MGB. Both models have become classic British sports cars.

(above) The 1958 MGA Coupe was instantly popular and is now considered a classic.

(below) Ferraris were originally built for racing. The first production Ferraris could be purchased only from the factory rather than from a dealership.

Ferrari: The Prancing Horse

Ferrari is one of the most famous makers of race cars and high-performance sports cars. It is an Italian brand of car that was founded by Enzo Ferrari in 1929. Production Ferraris, or Ferraris meant for the street, are meant to look and perform similar to racetrack Ferraris. They are wide and low to the ground, and were often painted stunning red, Italy's racing color. They are rare and often expensive cars that are built by hand in limited numbers.

Status Symbol: Porsche

Porsche is a very popular brand of high-performance sports cars. Ferdinand Porsche founded a company in 1931 in Germany, where it remains today. Porsche cars are known for their compact, low-to-the-ground design and powerful engines. Popular Porsche models include the Porsche Boxster and the Porsche 911. The name Boxster is a combination of the words "boxer," which describes its box-shaped engine, and the word "roadster," a sporty, compact, two-seater convertible.

(above) The Porsche Carrera GT is Porsche's most powerful car. Very few are made every year and its main rivals are expensive models such as the Enzo Ferrari. It features a high-horsepower V10 engine.

Raging Bull: The Lamborghini

(above) The Murciélago is built for speed. It features a spoiler that can be adjusted for better airflow over the car, and side windows that fold in for greater aerodynamics. Side air scoops automatically adjust to let cool air into the engine for better performance.

Lamborghini cars were first built in 1963 under founder Ferruccio Lamborghini, whose company was famous for its tractors. Lamborghini cars are extremely fast and are built in limited numbers. Some models have gull wing doors, which open up like a bird's wings. Lamborghinis also feature a flat design so that wind can flow easily over the top and help the car go faster. Popular models of the Lamborghini include the Diablo, Countach, and the rare Murciélago.

The Convertible

A convertible is a car with a roof that can be open or closed. The roof is either folded back into a rear compartment by hand or it is operated mechanically. One type of roof is made from cloth, plastic, or vinyl and is called a soft-top. The other type is made from a rigid material such as metal or fiberglass.

The First Convertibles

In the early 1900s, most cars did not have windows or roofs. Enclosed models, known as sedans or hardtops, became popular in the mid-1920s, and that style has remained popular. Power roofs that can be opened and closed mechanically by pressing a button were introduced by Plymouth in 1939. Convertibles first became popular in the 1930s. Today, many models of cars are available as convertibles, so drivers can choose between an open or closed ride.

(below) This hot pink Cadillac Eldorado convertible was built in 1959. Its oversized tail fins were popular at the time.

(below) The first Ford Thunderbird was made to rival the Chevrolet Corvette. It had a powerful V8 engine, two doors, and came standard with a soft-top. Later models like this 1963 Thunderbird were much larger and also came as hardtops.

Stand Out In The Crowd

Owners of convertibles like their cars because they are eye-catching and attractive. Drivers can experience the speed of the car by feeling the wind. Lower-priced convertibles are a good alternative for people who want a flashy car, but cannot afford a luxury or high-end sports car.

The first roadsters were convertibles without side windows, but most modern versions have power windows, like this Z4 Roadster from BMW.

(below) This red hot ride is the MX5, or Miata from Mazda. It is small, handles well, and is fun to drive.

Warm Air and Sunny Skies

Convertibles are ideally suited to warm climates because they can be enjoyed year-round. Hollywood movies have helped make convertibles seem glamorous. Popular models of convertibles in the past have included the Ford Thunderbird, the Lincoln Continental, and the Chrysler LeBaron. Popular models today include the BMW Z4, the Porsche Boxster, and the Beetle convertible from Volkswagen.

Almost any car can be turned into a sweet ride by adding a convertible option. This Volkswagen Beetle has a soft-top that folds back and is snapped into place.

Sport-utility Vehicles

Sport-utility vehicles, or SUVs, are large vehicles designed to go off-road and haul large loads. SUVs made by luxury car companies such as Cadillac, Porsche, BMW, and Lincoln, are sweet rides with expensive price tags.

Lugging Loads

SUVs did not start out as sweet rides. As early as the 1930s, bigger vehicles that could carry many people or large loads were called "carryalls," or station wagons, because they were used to pick up travelers and their luggage at train stations. These vehicles were also made for traveling over rougher roads, and were not seen as luxurious rides. Today, sweet SUVs are replacing these older models.

(above) The Land Rover was first made for traveling over rough terrain. The modern Land Rover also allows owners to customize their vehicles with different luxury accessories.

SUVs like this Range Rover often have a hitch for attaching trailers or other equipment.

A Vehicle with a View

Modern SUVs are popular for their large size, stylish appearance, and ability to go anywhere. SUVs are often symbols of wealth and status. Many people like SUVs because they are higher off the road than regular cars, giving the driver greater visibility. SUVs include four-wheel drive, where all four wheels work to drive the vehicle rather than just the front or back two, as in many other cars. This helps SUVs handle better in poor weather.

The Range Rover Sport offers the best performance and style from Land Rover.

Woodie Wagons

Woodie wagons are wooden bodied station wagons that were made from the late 1920s to the early 1950s. They were considered to be very stylish at the time. They were popular with families, and later with surfers in California, who needed to haul large boards to the beach.

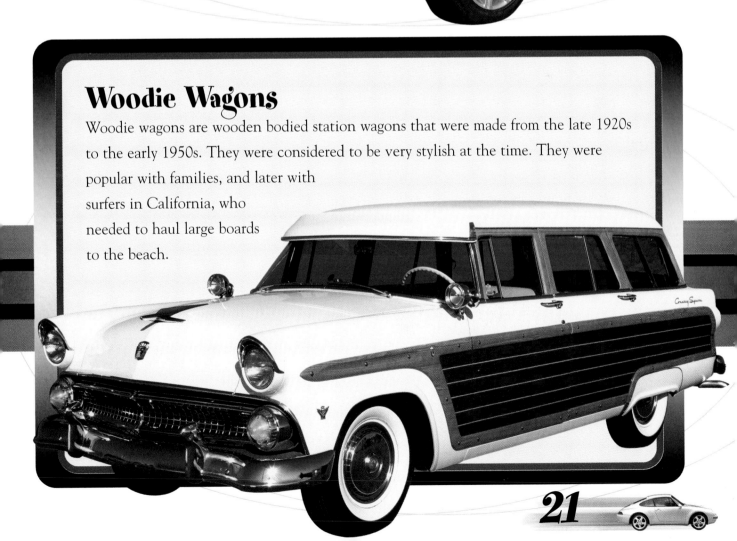

Sweet as Pie

Luxury SUVs feature all of the accessories of luxury cars, but perform like trucks and can go off road. Sweet SUVs, such as the Porsche Cayenne, have the same power and smooth ride as a Porsche sedan, but have much more space. Their interiors are large and luxurious, and they often have heated leather seats, global positioning systems, and television screens for passenger viewing. Some celebrities customize their SUVs with special details, such as stamping their names onto the wheel rims.

(above) When released in 2002, the Cadillac Escalade was known as the world's most powerful SUV.

(below) The Cadillac Escalade EXT features the hauling ability of a pickup truck, the seating capacity of a SUV, and the accessories of a luxury car.

Hum-Vee

High Mobility Multi-Purpose Wheeled Vehicles, or HMMWVs, are used by the United States Military for carrying troops and equipment, and they can also be used as ambulances, fire trucks, and other emergency vehicles. Hum-Vees, as they are nicknamed, are suited for military use because of their reliability and durability. Four-wheel drive allows for better handling off-road.

The H2 Hummer comes with three different option packages. The most luxurious one has DVD systems for back seat passengers.

Street Hummer

(above) The 2006 Jeep Commmander Limited comes with a huge V8 engine, and an optional global positioning system.

The street version of the HMMVW is called the Hummer. It was first sold to the public in 1992. It comes in three versions, the H1, H2, and H3. The H1 is the largest model and looks very similar to the military version. The H3 is the newest and smallest Hummer and is built more for city driving. Hummers look tough and have many luxury features, including heated seats and loud, clear sound systems. Buyers can customize their Hummers by choosing the color of body paint and interior, **trim package**, and other accessories. Features such as leather interiors and **automatic transmissions** come with hefty price tags.

The Limousine

Limousines are long, luxurious vehicles that are usually rented for a short period of time rather than purchased. Limousines are used for special occasions, such as weddings.

A Closed Ride

The limousine originated in France. The first limousines were covered horse-drawn carriages where the chauffeur, or driver, sat outside of the coach. The word limousine was also first used in America to describe enclosed, gas-powered cars operated by chauffeurs in the early 1900s.

(above) An early limousine from 1914. Limousines at this time were covered vehicles that were driven by a hired driver.

Big Band Buses

The first stretch limousine featuring an extra long body was built in Fort Smith, Arkansas, in 1928. The vehicles became popular with celebrities, politicians, and musicians. The extra-long cars earned the nickname "big band buses" because they could fit a musical band, including the musicians, plus all of their equipment and instruments, in one car. The earliest car companies to make limousines were luxury carmakers, such as Rolls-Royce, Duesenberg, Pierce-Arrow, and Lincoln. Today, **restored** vintage limousines, such as the Rolls-Royce Silver Cloud, are popular for special events.

(left) By the 1920s, Hollywood stars were driven to and from work in limousines.

Living Large

Limousines are made by many different luxury carmakers today. The Hummer limousine is large enough to fit more than 20 people. The insides of some customized Hummer limos feature hardwood floors, dance-floor lighting, bars, casino tables, and entertainment centers with **plasma televisions**, and deluxe stereo sound systems. Some limousines even include hot tubs. Ten-person Cadillac CTS and Jaguar limousines feature flat-screen televisions and wooden cabinets filled with crystal glasses. SUV limos fit 24 people or more. The Ford Expedition limo even has marble floors!

(below) Hummer stretch limos feature video game systems and leather interiors.

(above) This 72-foot (22-meter) limousine seats 38.

(below) Modern limousines have many accessories, such as televisions and mini refrigerators.

25

Retro Rides

A retro ride is a car that has been designed to resemble a model from the past. Retro rides are often more luxurious than the original versions, feature new accessories, and offer better performance.

The Best Kind of Bug

The original Beetle debuted in Germany in 1938 and was designed by car engineer Ferdinand Porsche. The idea was to build a quality, affordable family car. The name Volkswagen means "the people's car," and the Beetle was named after its distinctive, bug-like shape. Its engine is in the back of the car, rather than in the front.

The Comeback Beetle

The original Beetle was popular because it was reliable and affordable, but it was not considered a sweet ride at the time. The New Beetle was introduced as a **concept car** in 1994 and went into regular production in 1998. It was a modernized version of the old Beetle. The engine was now in the front of the car, and many aspects of the car were updated. The New Beetle has some luxury features, such as a power sunroof, CD and **MP3** stereo, and heated seats. It is also available in a convertible version.

(top right) Bug owners proudly display their cars in a parade.

(right) The New Beetle featured at a car show in Detroit, Michigan.

(left) The PT Cruiser is modeled after sedans from the 1930s.

(below) The Silver Arrow from Pierce-Arrow was made in 1933. It was an extremely rare and expensive vehicle at the time.

Old School: PT Cruiser

The PT Cruiser, released by Chrysler in 2001, is a modern car inspired by the styling of sedans from the 1930s. Cars of this time period had small windows and fenders with running boards. Running boards are panels that run along the sides of a vehicle. Passengers can place their feet on the panels to help them get in and out of the vehicle. The PT Cruiser hints at some of the automotive design elements from this era. It comes in both convertible and enclosed versions. It has several options, including a power sunroof, customized floor mats, and chrome accents.

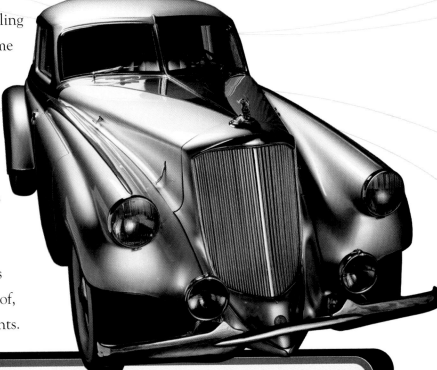

Sun and Moon

A sunroof is an opening in the roof of a car where the metal has been cut out and turned into a lid. It opens to let light and air in. A moonroof is a panel of glass in the roof of a car that lets light in. Sometimes, moonroofs have extra panels on the interior that can slide across and cover the glass. Adding a sunroof or a moonroof adds instant sweetness to a vehicle, but it comes with a price.

Cute and Small: The Mini

The Mini Cooper made its debut in 1959. The car, made by a manufacturer called the British Motor Corporation, became famous for being a tiny car with a powerful engine. The car also had a surprising amount of room inside. The Mini Cooper handled exceptionally well and was used for both racing and regular use.

The MINI Revamped

The Mini Cooper was redesigned in 2001, and became known as the MINI. It has the retro look of the early Mini, but is completely different inside. The new MINI is larger and includes features such as satellite radio, heated leather seats in a variety of colors, and heated exterior mirrors that prevent snow from collecting on them and obstructing the visibility of the driver. The new MINI gained widespread fame when it was featured in the 2003 movie *The Italian Job.*

(left) The new, fully loaded MINI is larger than the original version, features all-leather interiors, and is built for superior handling.

The new MINI (left) looks much like earlier versions of the car (above), but has updated technology to offer a comfortable ride. The MINI is available in convertible and enclosed versions.

The Mustang Reloaded

The original Mustang from Ford is considered a classic American sports car. It has gone through many design changes in its 40-year history. The redesigned 2005 Mustang includes many of the early Mustang's design features, with a modern twist. It is considered a fastback because it has a short trunk with an angled back window. The new Mustang has a long hood, and a front grille that is made to resemble Mustangs from the 1960s. The new Mustang also comes with a high-horsepower engine and leather seats that are available in a variety of colors.

The 2005 Mustang (right and below) was inspired by earlier versions of the car, which debuted in 1964 (above). Mustangs created the new pony car class.

Behind the Machines

Sweet rides combine elegant style and impressive performance. They have a lasting legacy and timeless beauty. The visions of talented, creative designers resulted in some of the sweetest rides ever made.

Style & Substance: Harley Earl

Harley Earl is one of the most famous American car designers. Earl began his career by designing cars for movie stars and other celebrities. He was later hired by General Motors (GM) to bring a new style to their cars. Earl made some of the most beautiful and outrageous concept cars of the 1950s at GM. He believed that a car's style was as important as its function and he made this idea a priority in all the cars he created. Two of Earl's most famous and stylish cars were the 1938 Buick concept car, called the Y Job, and the Chevrolet Corvette. The Corvette has remained popular for over 50 years and its long-lasting success is one of Earl's greatest legacies.

(below) Harley Earl stands next to the Firebird XP-21, a single-seater concept car that he designed. Earl made his cars longer and lower to the ground. He thought this design was more appealing to the eye.

Racing In His Blood: Enzo Ferrari

Enzo Ferrari is the founder of the famous race car brand Ferrari. Originally interested in car racing, Ferrari built his career around creating the ultimate racing machine. Ferrari continues to make race cars, but also make production Ferraris, which are among the most admired and sought-after cars in the world. Ferrari's lasting legacy is one of speed and excellence in design.

(left) Enzo Ferrari testing his Alfa-Romeo car. His race car-inspired designs remain popular today.

Quality and Innovation: Ferdinand Porsche

Ferdinand Porsche is remembered for the stylish sports cars that bear his name. His early years were marked by consistent inventions and innovations. Porsche impressed sports cars fans when he developed the Mercedes-Benz SSK in 1928. The SSK was considered the fastest sports car in the world when it debuted. In 1931, he was hired to create a high-quality, affordable "car for the people." He created the Volkswagen Beetle, which was an instant success.

Ferdinand Porsche (middle) is remembered for his innovations in car design that ranged from the super fast Mercedes-Benz SSK to the reliable Volkswagen Beetle.

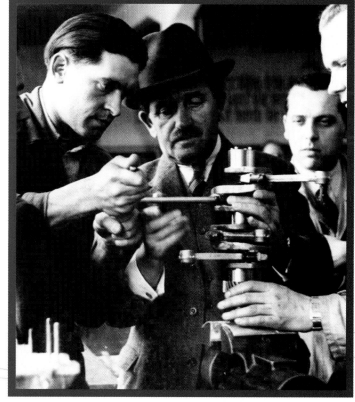

Glossary

aerodynamic A design that allows air to move over, under, and around a car better

assembly line A series of workers that perform specific tasks to put something together

automatic transmission A system for gears to change without the driver's assistance

chrome A shiny coating, of the metal chromium

concept car A car that is made to display design ideas for a possible future model

convertible A car with a roof that can be opened or closed

customize To make adjustments to a car to suit the owner's taste

dealership A place where cars are purchased

decal A design that is applied to a surface

export To send goods to another country for sale

fenders Guards over the wheels of a vehicle

fiberglass A material made of fine glass particles

global positioning system (GPS) A computer that gives drivers directions to their destinations

Great Depression A period from 1929 to the late 1930s when the world's economy was poor

grille Metal grates at the front of a car that allow cooling air under the hood to cool the engine

hardtop A roof made of a hard material

horsepower A measure of how much energy an engine can produce

inflatable Requiring air to take shape

MP3 Computer files that carry music

plasma television A television with a flat screen that displays bright colors

ration A fixed amount of something such as sugar or gasoline, distributed during war when supplies are short

restore To bring an object back to its original condition so that it appears brand new

satellite radio A radio that receives stations from further distances than regular radios

sedan A four- to six-person vehicle

suspension The system of springs that helps cars handle bumps in the road

trim package Accessories and styling details

V8 An engine with eight cylinders arranged in a compact V-shape

World War II A global conflict fought from 1939 to 1945

Index

32